Shells

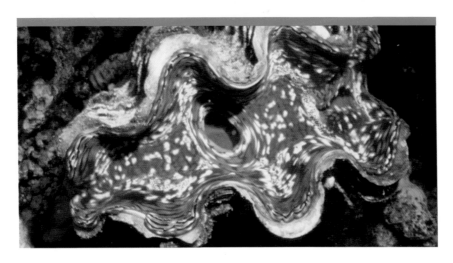

Lesley Pether

Look at this shell. A **snail** is inside this shell.

2

Sometimes, part of the **snail** is outside the shell.

The shell helps keep the **snail** safe.

4

The shell moves with the **snail**.

5

Look at this **crab**.
It has a shell.

The **crab** lives inside the shell.

The shell helps keep the **crab** safe.

The shell moves with the **crab**.

Look at this shell. A **clam** is inside this shell.

The shell helps keep the **clam** safe.

Look at this shell. A **turtle** is inside this shell.

Sometimes part of the **turtle** is outside the shell.

13

The shell helps keep the **turtle** safe.

The shell moves with the **turtle**.

Snail

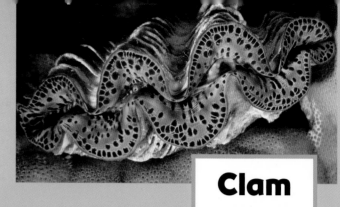

Clam

Crab

Turtle

These animals cannot live without their **shells**.
Their **shells** help keep them safe.